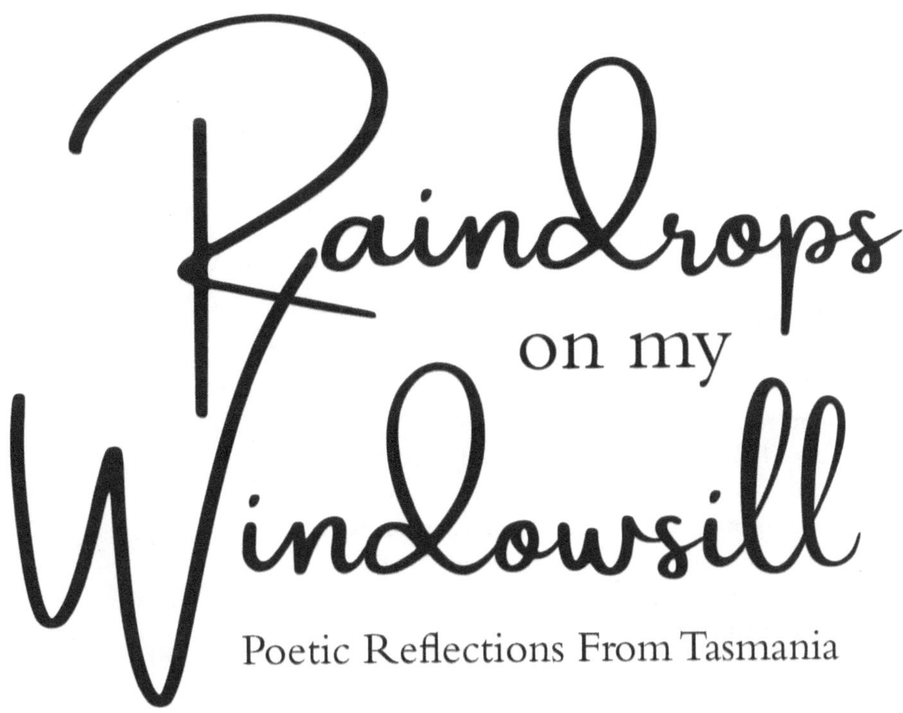

Raindrops on my Windowsill

Poetic Reflections From Tasmania

LESLIE HENDER

Raindrops on My Windowsill
Copyright © 2024 by Leslie Hender

All rights reserved. No part of this publication may be
reproduced, distributed, or transmitted in any form or by
any means, including photocopying, recording, or other
electronic or mechanical methods, without the prior
written permission of the author, except in the case of
brief quotations embodied in critical reviews and certain
other non-commercial uses permitted by copyright law.

Tellwell Talent
www.tellwell.ca

ISBN
978-1-77962-111-5 (Hardcover)
978-1-77962-110-8 (Paperback)
978-1-77962-112-2 (eBook)

To my wife, Wang Yi Juan (June), whose love and understanding have been my greatest inspiration. This book is a testament to our journey together.

Table of Contents

Lutruwita's Embrace

In the heart of the wild Southern Sea,
lies a magical island, windswept and free.
Where mountains rise, shrouded in mist,
and the lure of nature is hard to resist.

Waving fields of lavender with their purple hue,
thrive under cloudless skies of duck-egg blue.
Wildlife freely roams, unbound and untamed,
on this island of beauty, widely proclaimed.

Huon pine whisper in the scented breeze;
ancient forests with their towering trees.
Raging rivers carve their timeless course,
powerful reminders of nature's force.

In Lutruwita's heart, where cool winds blow,
stands Cradle Mountain, crowned with snow.
A sentinel of time, both fierce and grand,
guarding the secrets of this ancient land.

Cradle Mountain's lofty, rugged peaks,
echo past tales when the land speaks.
Lakes that reflect skies of azure blue
invoke memories, both old and new.

Glacial lakes, like mirrors, pure and clear,
reflect tall peaks that soar so near.
Buttongrass moorlands stretch far to the west,
a tapestry of wonders—nature's best!

Moss-covered forests, so lush and so green,
hiding shy thylacine few claim to have seen.
Echidna, platypus, and wombats freely roam
in their idyllic surroundings, their pristine home.

Tasmania, an island of unsurpassed delight,
a unique place to visit by day or by night.
From Hobart's bustle to Launceston's grace,
Lutruwita promises a warm embrace.

2

The Fool on the Rock

Rain falls effortlessly from the grey sky.
Sitting on a granite rock, an old fool is getting wet.
He doesn't seem to care; he just looks to the horizon,
Raindrops dripping from his face like cold sweat.

His thinning hair, like the sky, is grey.
Rain runs in rivulets down his sodden face.
His gaze intensifies as thunder rumbles closer,
As he sits on a rock in the rain in that mournful place.

The air is filled with bucolic smells:
The odour of sheep with a hint of wallaby,
Wood smoke with the unmistakable scent of pine drifting by.
Unbearable cold grips him; he shivers constantly.

He tries to forget the painful memories.
Some are fading; some are stronger than ever.
He shifts uncomfortably on his wet rock:
They seem hell bent on haunting him forever.

He pauses to wipe the rain from his tired face.
It's time, I think, to head back to the shack
To dry myself in front of a roaring wood fire.
It's time this old fool was heading back …

Anthophobia

My garden is overflowing with roses.
They say my blooms deserve a prize,
But what I am compelled to expose is ...
My roses are actually spies!

My garden is inundated with roses
Of all shapes and colours—what a sight.
But the one fact I must disclose is ...
They whisper about me at night!

You may think I'm totally demented,
But they watch me as close as can be.
Don't think this a story I've invented ...
They think I don't know, but I plainly see!

I hear them whispering about me
As they watch with envious eyes.
I pretend I can't hear them or see ...
What they say about me is all lies!

The roses in my garden are spying on me;
I hope you will believe what I say.
They are all determined to get me ...
I fear they will do for me one day!

They should not whisper about me
And laugh when my anguish occurs.
One night when they can't see me ...
I'll behead them with my secateurs!

Cosmic Conflict

Long, long ago, the Sun and the Moon had a fight.
The Sun turned bright red, the Moon a silvery grey.
Both believed that they were the brightest,
And the planets joined in the fray.

Their bitter fighting shocked the cosmos;
The Milky Way looked on in alarm.
The planets Mars, Venus, and Mercury
Begged all involved not to do any harm.

This cosmic conflict arose out of nothing.
The planets tried hard to understand
Why the Sun and Moon were quarrelling …
This was not what the Universe had planned!

Jupiter was asked to sit in judgement.
Twice the size of all the planets combined,
Jupiter thought on the subject for ages,
And then told all what was on its mind.

"In my opinion, this argument is trivial;
They each have nothing to gain.
Each thinks themselves the brightest:
Both the Sun and the Moon are vain.

The brightest is the Sun, in my judgement,
So, the Sun shall be radiant by day.
The Moon shall be brightest at nighttime;
On this subject, I have no more to say."

The argument was finally over.
Jupiter's judgement, all agreed, was quite right;
That's why the Sun shines in the daytime,
And the Moon beams at night.

Phonophobia in Perpetuity

It
Starts
Slowly
A bracing beat
Steadily building up
Like some giant rhythmic heart
Pumping out its noisy dissonance
In the land of perpetual noise
It never falters nor misses a beat
A constant *thump thump thump thump*
A deadly dirge of dreadful decibels descends
The noise of morning traffic steadily rises to a roar
A constant drone causing hypersensitivity in many
A multitude of millions, the Asiatic cacophony continues
Construction sites contribute with constant crashing and clamor
Drilling and hammering shouting jack hammering and more drilling
An endless barrage of fireworks parades and funerals add to the din
Competing with the city's myriad of harsh and strident sounds
Innumerable motorbikes and scooters ceaselessly shriek and scream
Street vendors add to the cacophony yelling as they sell street snacks
A never-ending roar a throaty bellow which turns into a screaming howl
Lunchtime looms and now we can hear the incessant *chop chop chop*
As countless lunchtime cooks hack their way through a mountain of food
Household pets join in the maddening throng with yelping and yapping
Inconsiderate pedestrians shouting loudly into innumerable mobile phones
Motorbike taxis touting for business with multiple high-pitched horns
Chattering and babbling pedestrians gesticulating at high speed
A never-ending ever-present unending clamor of sound
Ceaseless unending unendurable painfully tortuous
The dreaded daily dirge of dreadful decibels
Long into the night until the roar gradually subsides
A momentary respite a gathering of strength

Resting momentarily until dawn
Cynically known as
the Great Wail of
China.

Fascinating Fuchsias

Trembling in a gentle summer breeze,
A gathering of fuchsias shivers timidly.
Basking in the semi-shade where they thrive,
Their happiness is boundless
And their beauty quite alive.

Parading their ballerina-like blooms;
Each is more enchanting and delightful than the last.
Soon the dancing and laughing commences,
Their tiny faces bewitching;
Their swaying charms the senses.

With their vigorous sepals and delicate petals,
They sparkle like a galaxy of precocious stars.
Some are dressed in scarlet and white,
Their vivid colours bringing joy;
Their exquisite forms delight.

Eye catching in all their splendour,
Dancing fuchsias bring us colourful delight.
With their radiant colours streaming,
Their happiness always infectious,
Their delicate faces positively beaming.

Fuchsias, the most elegant of flowers,
They delight the eye and gladden the heart.
Each delicate flower is a little cutie,
Their vivid colours so charming,
Their elegance a thing of dazzling beauty.

Leaving the Middle Kingdom

I'm finally leaving the Middle Kingdom and say goodbye with a kiss.
It's been fun while it lasted, but there are some things I won't miss.
I won't miss the swarms of people who push and shove one another.
I won't miss the swarming crowds, each
looking very similar to the other.
I won't miss the rules of the road which no driver obeys.
I won't miss the pollution or the choking haze.
I won't miss the constant noise from which there is no peace.
I won't miss the corruption or the ineffectual police.
I won't miss the motorbikes that swarm all the roads.
I won't miss the horn-blaring trucks carrying unsafe loads.
I won't miss scrawny chickens with their severed heads on a dish.
I won't miss those dreadful smells like the stench of cuttlefish.
I won't miss the pollution that gets in every pore.
I won't miss the spitting a horrible sound I abhor.
I won't miss the supermarkets that have little for the likes me.
I won't miss the shops that sell nothing but oolong tea.
I won't miss the traffic which, I swear, is totally insane.
I won't miss the drivers who speed in the wrong lane.
I won't miss pedestrian crossings where people get in the way.
I won't miss the thoughtlessness until my dying day.
But I will miss the smiling faces of the students that I taught.
I will miss their curiosity and friendship so eagerly sought.
For in all my time in China they were the very best part.
They will be with me always and forever in my heart.

Expectations

He staggered, more glumly than wearily,
Fell like a drunk … heavy as dead meat,
And no power on earth could get him to his feet.
He blinked blearily in the driving rain.
He didn't expect to get lost.
He didn't expect any danger.

I'm sure they will be searching for me now, he told himself.
The dense scrub tore at his clothes and skin,
Depleting and exhausting both body and soul.
Stunningly beautiful, the wilderness can also be unforgiving …
He didn't expect it would beat him.
He didn't expect any problems.

What started out as an adventure is now deadly serious.
Hopes were raised: they searched for days but found nothing.
Police said they held "grave fears," having seen no sign of him.
The search intensified … but not a trace of the bushwalker was found.
He didn't expect to tire so quickly.
He didn't expect to give up.

Months passed, and his crumpled backpack was eventually discovered.
A few steps further on, he lay where he had fallen,
A scattering of sun-bleached bones beside a grinning skull.
Foolhardy? You might very well think so …
He didn't expect any fear.
He didn't expect to die.

14

Good Bones

Houses can be like people:
Some are well treated, others not so.
Our current home was once seriously maltreated,
Abused, misused, trashed, thrashed,
But I was reassured she had good bones.
Broken window frames, cracked glass,
Shattered and punch-holed doors …
But she has good bones.

Mice infested, urine stained, grimed throughout:
Carpets torn and worn beyond salvage,
Dust-covered grime in all its hideousness.
Filthy, dirty almost beyond belief,
Rotting floorboards, the musty smell of damp.
Missing doors, broken glass panes,
And a stench that came direct from hell …
But she has good bones.

Garden hideously overgrown:
Fallen fences, unkempt greenery,
Grass as long as your arm.
Discarded car tyres, an assortment of junk,
Garbage piled up in a putrid heap.
The house looked gloomy and cold
As it stood alone, surrounded by trash.
A pathetic, deplorable sight …
But she has good bones.

Enter plumbers, electricians, and builders:
A magical makeover in the offing.
New windows, new doors,
A spanking, brand-new bathroom.

Leslie Hender

New carpets, new light fittings,
New plumbing, new electrics,
A miraculous resurrection, a beautiful home …
And all because she had good bones!

Silent Sentinels

Not far from heart of an ancient Chinese capital
Stands a silent army, patiently awaiting the call.
High cheeked, in neat formation, faces set in clay;
Guardians of the Emperor stand silent and tall.

The Emperor dreamed of celestial rule,
Guarded by clay warriors and their bronze weaponry.
The Terracotta Warriors, buried for an eternity,
Guardians of an Emperor's unending legacy.

Each face unique; etched by skilled hands,
Crafted from clay, their resolve deftly imbued.
Row upon row, they stand in formation,
A silent army in loyal servitude.

Hollow eyes stare out from the distant past.
Strong and sturdy warriors, each in their prime.
Bowmen, infantrymen, all with unwavering loyalty;
Each sworn to serve the Emperor for all time.

At their sides hang polished bronze swords.
Armour gleaming, they stand, eternally dreaming
Of bloody battles consigned to ancient history;
Each man steadfastly loyal and unwavering.

In Xi'an's ancient earth, they patiently wait,
Echoing the battle cries of campaigns hard fought,
For they embody the spirit of an ancient land
And the unification of China the Emperor sought.

These clay warriors have withstood the test of time;
Now, one of the world's greatest spectacles,
Their spirit endures throughout the centuries.
The Terracotta Warriors, silent sentinels.

Intermingling

Beware the sweet intermingling of memories,
Which can often waft across an introspective mind.
By examining our own sensory and perceptual experiences,
We can sometimes find a peace of a kind.

Listen to the enveloping music as it transforms us,
Transports us to a soothing, magical place;
A place we've never been to but long to go,
An enchanted, captivating world filled with sweet grace.

Beware the sweet intermingling memories of love,
Which will often entrap and ensnare our dreams.
If we dare to linger too long, we are lost,
And our understanding of life is not what it seems.

Listen to the sound of love as it takes us away,
Away from the burden of desolate reality
To drift where few have been, until we finally
Sit silently in the cooling shade of some majestic tree.

A Serious Social Issue

A huddle of grubby clothes lies on the pavement.
Inside them, shivering and afraid, is an unkempt man.
Bearded, shivering, and covered with ingrained dirt,
Trying to stay warm, trying to stay alive anyway he can.

A mother's son, his former life is but a distant memory
As he shambles through his wretched life, all hope faded.
Hungry, tired, and emphatically frightened of life,
His negative view of the world understandably twisted and jaded.

His life is dangerously off course; he lacks direction,
Stumbling blindly through each bitterly cold day,
Begging for spare change, his future past,
This pathetic huddle of grubby clothes shuffles on his way.
hat a fellow human being should live in hopelessness,
It should fill us all with anger, resentment, and rage.
We owe it to ourselves to put an end to homelessness.
How can this be in this modern day and age?

Recalcitrant Child

This is for you, my child,
It comes from my loving heart.
It is for you, my long-lost daughter,
The first beloved child of an ill-fated marriage.
Now, I am growing old, a shadow of my former self.
I think of you and how you once were
And all the fatherly love I had for you.
What have you become now?
No longer a child,
You are now a woman, a mother
Who also had an ill-fated marriage.
There is much we have in common,
And yet, many long years have passed
Since I lost you. You, who did not hesitate
To sever the bonds between father and child.
I was a kind and loving father;
You know this is undeniable.
I often wonder what kinds of demons dwell in your heart.
Are these the same demons that possess your mother?
I wonder.
At night, I often think about you.
I think of all the love that was lavished upon you;
I think of the love that was never reciprocated,
How manipulative you were,
And how you hectored your sister with cruel callosity.
You have children I have never met.
Do they love their mother?
Will they sever their bonds with you, as you did me?
For your sake, I hope not.
For the pain inflicted by a recalcitrant child
Is more painful than you can possibly imagine.

Transported

They struggled through life's bloody mud.
The mud that stuck each time they smiled,
And each time they wiped away the blood,
Remembering the love of a long-lost child.

Life was tough, but they did not care.
They struggled on, but with hope bereft
Life became a dangerous game of dare,
Until, one day, they were accused of theft.

Caught by the law, they stood in fear
Like foxes trapped in the light of the moon,
And soon it all became abundantly clear:
What had happened had come all too soon.

The law punished with such resentment.
Make an example, came the crowd's outraged howl.
Sentence was pronounced with such contentment,
For a crime they thought so heinous and foul.

To Van Diemen's Land, you will be sent on ships
Where your punishment will be at the court's discretion.
Anguished cries erupted from their lips:
Seven years transportation for their transgression.

Taken in chains to the Portsmouth slips,
Each one knew they had to stay strong.
Together they boarded those accursed ships,
Transported down under for what they'd done wrong.

Life had been good, a thing of beauty.
But now, torn from their beloved homeland,
They suffered in silence, as was their duty,
Until finally they arrived in Van Diemen's Land.

They came to Port Arthur, the Devil's lair.
They were placed in darkness, each in their cell.
Life was cheap; the authorities didn't care,
And life was hard in Van Diemen's Hell.

They struggled through life's bloody mud.
The mud that stuck each time they smiled,
And each time they wiped away the blood,
Remembering the love of a long-lost child.

The Short-Lived Poet

A long life was not for him;
He became a poet, acting on a whim.
Luckily, he was not at all adverse
To writing poems verse by verse.

He wrote of love and broken hearts,
Went to Oxford and studied fine arts.
He worshipped from afar his ladylove
And wrote of romance and cherished love.

Then, off to France to fight the Hun;
It'll be over by Christmas, Oh what fun!
Two pips upon his shoulders broad,
War has come, unsheathe the sword!

The guns roared, trenches were dug,
But the dreamer was a silly young mug.
Mud and blood: a baptism of fire,
No more quenching love's desire.

Killed instantly by a whizzbang, what a shame.
Now, hardly anyone remembers his name.
He died so fast he didn't even know it,
And that was the end of the short-lived poet!

Night Market

Plying the fruits of their labour, vendors jostle
Under the humid night sky of a warm July evening.
A sea of faces and the unmistakable aroma of China
Announce that the night markets are open for business.
The traders optimistically set up their flimsy stalls,
In the hope they will make many sales.
Now that night has fallen, they will cast their nets,
Selling cheap clothing and poor-quality shoes.
Making a living here isn't easy,
But at least they know they'll eat tonight.
The streets throb with expectancy and longing,
Scooters weaving nimbly from side-to-side dart back and forth.
Teenage girls flex their legs, wearing their high-tension smiles
While besotted boys watch the girls with high cheekbones
As they head towards an all-night eatery for noodles.
The smell of grilled meat blends with the stench of durian,
A fruit that smells like hell but tastes like heaven.
The traders with renewed optimism promenade their wares,
Their shrunken, expectant faces always hoping for a sale,
False smiles painted firmly on their faces
While the teenage girls look on through half-closed eyes,
Homeward-bound shoppers always looking for a bargain.
And then, in the early hours of the morning,
The traders pack up their flimsy stalls
To try again the next night.

Willy Willy

A playful hot wind blows across the land
Unfettered and unchecked by any obstruction,
Impishly stirring the hot sun-baked sand,
Fully intent on its course of destruction.

Bushies scratch their heads in disbelief
At the sight of tortured trees bent double
As the upward-spiralling wind spreads its grief,
Gathering its strength and intent on trouble.

The Willy Willy is a destructive scourge of nature;
A demonic dust devil filled with evil intent,
Howling like some hideous demonic creature,
An unstoppable wind, impossible to prevent.

The dust devil whirls and swirls, a menacing sight;
The air is filled with dust and debris.
The wind is strong, nothing stays upright
As the dust devil sweeps along, howling like a banshee.

"There's a wild dust devil coming!" they all yell
As the Willy Willy rapidly approaches,
An angry wind coming straight from hell.
"Quickly, take cover!" an urgent voice reproaches.

The dust devil swirls with a ghostly howl;
It lashes viciously at the tortured trees.
It attacks us in an assault most foul,
Determined to bring us to our knees.

We shut the windows and lock the doors;
People cower like frightened mice.
The rafters shake, and we shelter indoors
As the wicked wind lashes the house.

It screams and howls like an army of ghosts,
And our fences are fair blown away,
Leaving nothing but the twisted posts
Looking unearthly, like grotesque feet of clay.

A group of once-proud sycamore
Lays flattened and awkwardly awry,
While all around looks like a bloody war,
And all we can do is cry.

The house which has stood for a hundred years
Has lost its terracotta tiles.
The loss of our roof drives us to tears,
As the wind blows our property for miles.

Now, winds come, and winds go,
But this dust devil wind wanted to stay.
For many an hour it continued to blow,
And all we could do was pray.

But then it must have changed its mind
And headed away to the east.
The Willy Willy was anything but kind,
And we were glad to see the back of the beast.

Where did the Willy Willy come from?
Where will the Willy Willy go?
Why is a Willy Willy so destructive?
I guess we'll never know …

Raindrops on my Windowsill

I fell into the honey pot, more or less on purpose;
Primitive urges compelled me to instinctive actions.
From that day forward, the die was cast,
And I considered the rain and your reactions.

Effortlessly, the rain fell, turning from drizzle to downpour.
The windows were dotted with limpet-like raindrops;
The sturdy green window frames rattled in the wind.
I will look for your reaction, but only when the rain stops.

Your eyes are fixed like raindrops on my windowsill;
You pout like a child as the wind shrilly whistles.
The rain is drumming rhythmically on my window still,
While your perplexing and intense anger bristles.

I sense your anguish as the weather intensifies;
The rain is now falling like the tears you cry.
The world is now watching us as the rain finally fades,
And the sun watches us with its golden eye.

32

Secret Desire

I often think of you, my secret desire …
Especially in the morning, when it's you I crave.
Your erotic aroma fills the room;
You and you alone are the object of my desire.
You are fruity, smooth, and tactile;
I passionately anticipate your delights.

You are so unimaginably desirable …
My cravings are strong—I must have you.
Religiously, each and every morning,
I grind you down.
You are pulverized and aromatic;
You are the object of my desire.

You are so incredibly hot …
You lie there waiting for me,
Spiralling, beguiling, seducing me.
You are sweet like toffee;
You are delectably desirable.
Oh, how I love my morning cup of coffee!

Summer Nights

I often think of those tranquil summer nights—
When time froze and the seasons stood still;
Hot, sultry days when the earth was warm,
And the moon shivered in frozen silence.

We strolled each evening over sand-covered beaches …
And a million stars twinkled with sheer delight
As we cheekily kicked off our sandals
And screamed our delight at the Milky Way.

The years have quickly caught up with us—
We have been overtaken by modern technology.
Too old to be saved, too young to die,
And now eating meat makes us nauseous.

We saw and did many truly amazing things …
Standing there at the edge of the universe,
A reflective moon, shoals of fish, and the ever-foaming surf,
Way back when, during those cool summer nights.

Lying, as we did each evening, next to a seething surf—
A thousand pairs of eyes watched inquisitively
And assumed our perfect innocence
While we swam in an ocean of love.

Under swaying palm trees, we lived and loved life …
Mother Nature took us to her heart.
Saying farewell to our shared memories, we let go and swam away,
Only to be dissolved in the murk of conformity.

I often think of those idyllic summer nights—
When time stood still, and the years fell away.
Now, on cold wintry days when the sun has turned to ice,
We sit together and shiver in frozen silence.

Bushfire

Long after the earth died, the old men cracked a smile.
Their toothless grins were as empty as any dried upriver—
Wrinkled, shrunken, devoid of emotion, mirthless, and corrupted.
The silent stones watched as the summer sun glared,
burning deep into the earth, scalding, blistering;
Where water once washed, the brown earth buckled and cracked.
Silent stones sweltering in the baking sun watched:
Their outcrops stood motionless, hanging in soft silence,
Watching the earth slowly die while the flames licked at the grass.
Soon, the grass was incinerated, then the trees, and then the animals.
Slowly at first and then faster until the crackle became a roar—
Asleep in their holes, lizards were baked alive
While still buried in their burrows; not a good way to die.
The earth turned black while fortune spared the living;
A hot wind fanned the blackened stumps, swirling and shifting.
After the flames had past, after the end of the world,
New life spluttered and germinated, feeding on the flesh of the dead.
Ash reigned supreme, blackened trees pointed agonisingly skyward,
And yet life had lingered, started anew, rejuvenated—
No longer a smoking ruin but a fresh opportunity at life.
The bush regenerated; life was jumping, a metamorphosis.
Quivering, shaking, trembling growth crawled back;
Life crawled out of death and slowly began again.
Insects inched their way back, young green leaves burst forth
And the grass saw the light and released their grip on darkness.
The bush regenerated, and the trees smiled once again
While the silent stones waited with anticipation—
Rain peppered the dry land, bringing life and growth;
Like a garden in spring, the bush sprang back, full of life.
The silent stones grinned softly ... they'd seen it all before.

Rattus rattus

Here's to the shadow of the rat,
Falling where it stood by the silent shadows,
A mutilated, bloody heap of death—
An effective death.
Life was hell, then came the end, a blessed relief.
At least it's over; the suffering has ended.

Heaven shudders and offers up a sigh;
Another sad creature has met a sticky end—
Vermin are never mourned.
Shrieking as it meets its untimely demise,
Incisors bared, threatening and defensive
As the Universe looks on in horror.

A loathed and detested species,
Rattus rattus was cursed
And will never be missed.
Never buried, never grieved;
The plague-bearing rat got a bum rap—
The rat is dead; long live the rat!

Accused of spreading the bubonic plague,
But the fleas and lice were spread by humans, not rats.
The Black Death has no face.
Bubonic plague wasn't down to rats;
It wasn't God's punishment.
It wasn't *Rattus rattus*—
Rattus rattus is innocent!

Reflections at the Edge of the World

I stand at the edge of the world looking south.
The southern wind whips at me remorselessly;
Both feet are planted firmly on the sandy beach—
In front of me lies the grey-green Tasman Sea.

I stand literally on the edge of the world.
Directly ahead of me lies the distant Antarctic;
Above me frantic sea birds spin and whirl.
Being near the ocean, for me, is always cathartic.

The ocean thrashes and heaves before me,
Hurling itself angrily against the rocky shore.
The sea spray pelts my salt-encrusted face,
It is time to move on, to explore.

The salty air whispers secrets, as yet untold.
With each step I take on the seaweed-strewn sand,
My thoughts like ocean waves, rise and fall,
While the bitter southern wind tears across the land.

I pick my way steadily along the isolated shore,
Remembering Mawson who sailed south on the *Aurora*
To explore and make scientific observations;
Douglas Mawson, heroic Antarctic explorer.

To the south, brooding in the frigid grey ocean
Lies Antarctica, its secrets slowly being unfurled.
Over six-thousand kilometres distant—
From where I stand at the edge of the world.

Survival Mode

Across a clearing, a deer crashes on—
Wide eyed, panic stricken,
Running desperately for the trees
Which beckon warmly, offering protective cover.
Going about its natural inclination
And catching the heady scent of deer,
A wolf anticipates a meal, it's mouth salivating.

The nostrils on the deer twitch,
Catching the unmistakably pungent odour of wolf.
Terror enters the mind of the deer,
An instinct of survival.
There will be no feast in this forest.
Survival mode kicks in, the will to live;
Still standing, listening intensely.
A twig snaps—
Eyes pierce the darkness looking for movement.
The wolf smells the air.

Something is stirring quite close.
Darkness is closing in.
Cold and as delicate as the snow,
The wolf's nose once again sniffs the air.
Two smouldering eyes look urgently for movement

As soft paws tread faint prints into the snow.
Between trees, he stalks his prey
Which has fled swiftly into the shadows of the night—
There'll be no meal tonight.

Never Again

My brain aches, crammed as it is in my cranium;
Merciless thoughts machete their way through brain tissue.
Is this a nightmare; why is my brain screaming?
I'm lost in confusion; I must be dreaming …
Where am I?

Watching in the mirror while I pry open my eyes;
My mind is a blank with fleeting memories.
Moving incessantly, my spinning brain gives a cry.
What on earth happened, where am I …
What am I doing here?

The dreadful misery of realisation begins to grow;
I remember last night's pounding music, the laughing faces,
Music blaring with a continuous beat: *thump, thump, thump.*
Movement and rhythm: *jump, jump, jump.*
What the hell was I doing?

Flashing lights, intoxicating sounds streak across my mind;
I pause to think and shudder at the memories.
I struggle with thoughts which flow like cascading water
Falling downwards; I see the passionless passion of slaughter …
What happened last night?

I stumble past empty bottles, crushed empty cans of lager,
Ashtrays ugly with stubbed-out and crumpled cigarettes;
Dancing and drinking: *what was I thinking …*
Flashes of memories: *my God, I did some drinking!*
Is that why my head is spinning?

Slowly, my memory returns like a bad smell;
What a party, what a night of debauched revelry.
Hours of partying, hours of drinking—*I must be insane?*
My cluttered brain finally clears; so, until the next time …
Never again!

Celestial Journey

And so, we started our celestial journey,
Witnesses to the ever-flowing river of light,
We stood amazed at the myriad of stars, infinite and unknown.
We were all witnesses to a truly awesome sight.

Lost in a dazzle of brightly flickering lights,
We watched as the cosmos gently floated by;
We stood in wonder and hugged each other in delight
And marvelled as the flickering lights danced across the sky.

So distant and yet so close, space was now quite warm,
Then we saw a sign that we could all recognise.
A shower of glittering stars fell to earth and lay still,
Landing beside us, a precious gift from the skies.

We chatted excitedly like precocious children
And waded toward the sparkling stars now resting askew.
Approaching in awe, we drew close to the stars,
Which now sparkled with colours of turquoise and blue.

As the heavens slowly expanded and started to glow,
We blinked in the twilight and winked at the moon.
Solemnly, we stood there to observe the filtered light
And danced in the moonlight which ended all too soon.

Our bodies and souls separated, lifting us upwards.
Pure and imperishable, angelic and worthy,
Bathed in the light of a billion bright galaxies:
This was the end of our celestial journey.

Drought

A hot wind blows across the plain.
Dried blades of grass and assorted twigs
Tumble out of the east. *Bloody hot!*
Fiery heat. Miserable, dehydrated sheep.
Ewes caked crusty with dried mud,
Dying lambs sweltering under a merciless sun.
Miles of dry, barren land.
Two-hundred miles of parched farmlands. *Heartbreak!*
Bushfire smoke in the distance.
The baked ground writhes in a mirage of agony,
Burning like a stone-baked flatbread.
A pool of shimmering water appears,
A distorted optical illusion you'd swear was there,
Hovering just above the ground.
The birds are long gone, flown away.
Lizards nestle under cool rocks, shaded, comfortable,
While crows look on and groan.
The searing heat shows little sign of relenting.
Lamb's blood now soaks the dry earth.
Life is given up reluctantly.
The ewes can do nothing.
Wallabies hug the sparse shade of a few trees.
Survival is imperative.
Cockies seem invisible.
Smoking trees move a little closer;
Nervous ewes sniff the air, trembling,
Followed by the few surviving lambs.
The hot wind abates.
The precious rain finally returns,
Followed closely by the birds.
The smoke from the bushfire has gone;
New grass emerges.
The drought is over!

45

The Long Goodbye

Who is that woman who once loved and cared?
I refer to that elderly lady sitting quietly over there.
Why is she staring; why is she so scared—
She who once had freckles and bonny auburn hair …

When she was young, did she dream of love each night?
Or of being a mother who would raise children three;
Did she think of her future husband as some brave knight—
Or simply dismiss it as pure fantasy …

Who is that confused woman resting in the chair?
Why is her thinning hair so white and so long,
Why does she curse folk as if they don't care—
Now she is weak, but once she was strong …

In the cold light of dawn her hair's silvery grey;
This is the mother who has seen happier days.
Her body is thin as her life ebbs slowly away;
White, withered claws fumble as she piously prays.

Trying to remember a time and a place,
She looks in the mirror at her old, wrinkled eyes
And recoils from the sight of her own withered face
And sits in her armchair and quietly cries.

Her beauty has long passed; she's just skin and bone.
Precious memories have faded as the days pass by;
Soon she must pass, most likely on her own.
There's no time for regrets. Such a long goodbye.

Custodians

Vibrant are the sounds of life in nature;
Ears delight in the song of birds in the trees.
Eyes witness the glory of the Earth
And the spectacle of existence we all share.
Smile at us, but do not forget,
For we are the people of the land,
Custodians of the planet.
Listen to the voices that never cease:
Too many fat cats.
Too much greed.
The mighty dollar always comes first;
The world is richer and yet poorer by far,
For we have lost our way and will pay a terrible price.
There is hunger in our bellies but laughter in our eyes.
So, let's laugh and love as we have been taught,
And to hell with the future!
Only you know who we are,
Only you have yet to speak out.
The fine smiles and inane chatter rattle in empty spaces:
We listened but never heard.
We looked but didn't see.
The blood ran red as the water wars raged;
There was nothing but empty people under an empty sky.
The eyes of the world looked for a saviour; none came.
They burnt the houses of the non-believers,
Leaving nothing but blackened beams and ashes.
And the skies darkened, and the water dried up,
And still, we did not speak out.
Each alone until they died,
Unseen by strangers.
Out of sight, out of hope, and out of mind:
Custodians of a dying planet.

Grandma's Lemon Meringue Pie

You can ask, but I will never tell you
The secret of my grandma's famous pie—
Not just any ordinary pie
But her delicious Lemon Meringue Pie.

You can torture me with red-hot pokers;
You can beat me until I die—
But I will never divulge the secret
Of grandma's Lemon Meringue Pie.

It was passed on by my great-great-grandma,
Who lived for a hundred years—
I'll never tell you the secret,
Though you twist off both my ears.

You know the pie contain lemons,
And you know it has meringue,
But other than that, I'm saying nothing—
And you can all go hang!

For I have sworn to keep silent,
And no matter how hard you try—
You'll never learn the secret
Of Grandma's Lemon Meringue Pie.

Motherly Love

A gentle smile lit up the young face like a beacon;
The look of wonderment shone as brightly as any star,
The glimmering characteristics of birth and death,
Condemned from the very start to an inevitable end ...

Intrigued by the light of the sun, eyes look upward.
The pale signature of hope was there from the start,
Kindled in the womb and forged by genetic forces,
The love brimmed over and was accepted by the child.

And so, the bond was forged with blood and pain,
Marinated in life-long motherly love and devotion.
Burning brightly like the sun stars of the universe,
Heaven and hell both melded into one small world ...

The generous features as starry as the smile,
Imprinted forever on the loving face above.
That familiar smile, minted fresh as any coin,
The love that forever links the two inseparables.

A life yet to be lived will rise from this strong bond,
Abstracted from the void we struggle to understand.
There is no greater love, no love more intense,
Than the love of a mother for her child ...

You're Not To Blame

I watched you as you lay by my side,
Dreaming dreams of (what I hoped then) was me.
Troubled dreams, which you always denied;
Nightmares at times, you must agree.

Your dreams were dashed like breakers on a rock,
A troubled childhood full of dysfunction and fear.
For you, life came as a great big shock,
As you grew older the cracks began to appear.

I could see the vulnerability in your eyes,
(Like a love-sick fool, I was spellbound)
Blinded by love, I didn't see your disguise,
I could only see the love I was sure I had found.

The realisation came when it was far too late;
It came out of the blue like a thunderbolt.
My love withered but never turned to hate.
How could I blame you for what wasn't your fault?

Time has passed, and now I live a contented life.
(I hardly think of you at all these days)
I'm happily married to my second wife;
Life has moved on since we went our separate ways.

I can forgive that you never really loved me;
I can overlook all the suffering and pain;
I can excuse all the stress you gave me.
It's not easy to watch someone going slowly insane.

Incessant Rain

Pulsating across the wind-tormented fields, comes the rain,
Where wildlife wallow in the resultant flood.
Merciless, unforgiving rain drums its arrival on the roof,
Slashing at the windows and in league with the wind, rain sheets in.
Sheltering inside, we can only guess at the intensity outside,
Listening to the relentless pitter-patter as it pummels the roof.
Trees hang their miserable, soaking heads and wait,
Relentless rain splashing its silvery shower,
Drumming at walls and windows alike.
Pelting remorselessly.
The drumming intensifies, becomes a roar:
Water splashes, leaps, spins, soaks.
Every mutilated tree stands still, drooping under the onslaught,
Looking for all the world like a line of medieval
monks awaiting Armageddon.
The rain goes on and on incessantly;
Allied with the wind it changes tactics, attacking horizontally.
Windows are slammed shut,
Doors double checked, and ceilings scrutinised for leaks;
Puddles appear rapidly in the fields and streets.
Drains, engorged, are vomiting water.
The rain feels like it is winning and presses home the attack.
Burrows fill. Streams swirl and rivers rage.
With no respite from the storm, trees bend and buckle.
The world is awash and will soon drown;
The freezing rain soaks into every crevice.
The dark, angry clouds have shifted,
The drowning world gasps a breath
As the pouring skies slowly retreat …
The rain eases and stops.
Flicking its final contemptuous flurry at the sodden world,
Cursing its perceived defeat, it moves quickly away.
Vanishing, along with the brooding grey clouds.
Dogs shake themselves dementedly.
Incessant relief!

I Refuse to Grow Old

I refuse to grow old. I've made up my mind.
I don't want to shrink or find I've declined.
I don't want to wither and my face be all crinkly.
I refuse to grow old. I don't wanna be wrinkly.

I'd hate to grow old and have no adventures.
I don't want to have to wear dentures.
I want to live as long as Methuselah;
I don't want my hair fading to a grayish colour.

I refuse to grow old and breakfast on kippers.
I don't want to wear a sweater and a pair of slippers.
I wanna stay young and as fit as a fiddle.
I don't wanna use a commode when I gotta piddle!

I refuse to grow old and smell strongly of pee.
I want to stay alert, youthful, and free.
I plan to bypass old age, death, and dying.
I don't care that it's only to myself I'm lying.

As my life concludes, I know death is inevitable.
I hope and pray to God that I'm ineligible.
With a bit of luck, I'll simply drift away.
Good God in heaven, please, not today!

Fatigue Culturelle

Here, on foreign soil, my feelings of resentment brim over—
Simmering and brooding just below the surface for years.
This homesick nomad no longer wants to be a rover;
I must end my travels, bring an end to all my tears.

I'm tired of foreign travel, tired of being different,
Tired of cultural differences, and just tired of being tired.
Culture fatigue is messing with my head; I'm culturally indifferent.
It's time to pack my bags and leave; it's time this foreigner retired.

Time to evaluate my thoughts and take that homeward leap;
The rules I have lived by my whole life do not apply here.
I've often been pushed to breaking point; my anger goes deep—
It's time I left this foreign land; it's time to disappear.

Culture fatigue creeps quietly, slowly at first, then it hurries.
It will crush you if you stay too long in an alien nation.
You feel frustrated by even the smallest of worries;
Anger wells up at the slightest provocation.

Hyper-irritability and depression are signs of culture fatigue—
It's far too easy to blame others for your negative feeling.
Isolation and loneliness are complicit; they are in league,
Leaving you feeling vulnerable and your senses reeling.

You have no motivation, and you feel you've lost your identity.
You feel anxious and are unable to complete your daily tasks.
Your mind becomes twisted, each thought an obscenity;
You see your hosts as uncaring, hiding their thoughts behind masks.

You are preoccupied with your health and obsessively neat.
There's a sense of dread, a fear of being cheated or fleeced.
You are inordinately concerned over the safety of the food you eat—
You've long stopped pretending you enjoyed the feast.

It's time to pack your bags and head for home;
It's time to put an end to those baffling encounters.
Time to put an end to your desire to roam;
Shelve those negative feelings for out-of-towners.

55

Electric Blue

I fell out of bed and stumbled outside, half awake,
Out in the cold winter air, some fresh air to take.
I rubbed my eyes, dispelling sleep, and then
I heard the song of a tiny Fairy Wren.

As the sun came up, and the world was filled with light,
I heard the song of the Fairy Wren, to my right.
Singing loudly and calling in the early-morning glare
The reeling, high-pitched trill of notes they all share.

I stood transfixed, delighting in the wondrous sound,
Listening to their magical songs all around.
The shimmering males in electric shades of violet blue
Will sweetly sing to their eggs; I swear it's true.

Electric-blue feathers and a sky-blue cap,
The Fairy Wren is such a cheerful chap.
I'll be up early tomorrow, come rain or shine
And listen again for this newfound friend of mine.

Only a Memory

His mind stirs, slowly and methodically.
He recalls days from the distant past.
He thinks of young love and desire;
He thinks of hope and loss.
He struggles to remember some events
But recalls others in utter clarity.
Childlike, he giggles at a memory:
Those were the days.
His bony fingers shuffle old photographs,
Dog-eared, creased, and worn.
Black and white smiling faces,
Powerful memories flood back:
The confidence of youth.
But that was yesterday, long, long ago.
Challenges were eagerly accepted back then.
Sweating one minute and freezing the next,
Flushed, crimson faced, the gentle waft of perfume.
Stuttering embarrassingly:
Trying so very hard to impress.
It didn't really happen, though it was fun trying.
Bowed but never beaten.
Dazed but never despondent.
Their expressions set forever,
A fondness and an aching in his heart.
Standing in a hollow emptiness,
Modernity with all its cruelty reins:
Life is all but lost.
In a strange room of purplish emptiness,
Among new, meaningless phrases that confuse,
Among a scrapyard of elderly men and women,
Hobbling along on a forest of walking sticks:
Life is only a memory.

Elegance in Motion

When life ups the pressure and you run out of luck,
You should painfully drag yourself out of the muck.
If you want to be different; you must take a chance,
So, dance with the devil, or go into a trance!

Dance totally naked around your living room floor,
Pick a fight with your neighbour, that bastard next door.
Plan a cycling holiday to Holland or France,
Buy lots of bright clothes that scream *elegance*!

Shop till you drop in a New York boutique;
Buy a new outfit that's totally unique.
Smell every flower in the Botanical Gardens,
Or visit crooks who've received full pardons.

Cycle to Scotland, and eat a fresh kipper;
Drink China tea from a ceramic slipper.
Drink lots of lager at a Munich beer hall;
Climb the Matterhorn without having a fall.

Stuff your mattress with rolls of dollar notes;
Take up farming and breed Angora goats.
Try to be spirited and do take a chance:
Swim the Channel from England to France!

Run for President and tell lots of lies;
Take up cooking and make apple pies.
Swim to Jamaica and write a reggae song;
Tattoo your eyelids and grow your hair long.

Fish for sharks as you sail round the horn;
Tell the whole world where you were born.
Fly to North Korea and kiss Kim Jong-un;
Sail to Antarctica and bask in the sun.

Do lots of crazy things and don't hesitate;
Express your feelings as you search for a mate.
Elegance in motion should be your desire;
Live life to the full and then quietly retire!

59

Winter in Tasmania

Here in the Southern Hemisphere, it will be winter soon.
Autumn is fading; the long summer days, a blur.
Winter is upon us; it's now the beginning of June.
Icy winds from Antarctica are chillingly a-stir.

Autumn leaves have abandoned the trees.
We'll soon see the yellow bells of the daffodil,
Their heads nodding knowingly in the winter breeze,
Each cheerful flower bringing beauty and good will.

The pademelon, with its heavier and bushier fur,
Retreats gracefully into the scrubland mass
Or deep into the rainforest, which they prefer,
There to feed and wait for winter to pass.

Cradle Mountain in winter is truly delightful,
And clear nights are perfect for stargazing.
The freezing winds can, at times, be as frightful
As the lights of the Aurora Australis are amazing.

Snow from weeks ago still lingers on,
Outstaying its welcome like a partying reveller.
The cold winds sweep through the town pavilion,
And icy wind cuts deep as winter's messenger.

As falling snow dusts each eucalyptus tree,
Tasmania in winter is a place which, despite the cold,
Is a very special place and one you really need to see.
Tasmania in winter is a sight to behold.

The Tyranny of Plutocrats

Take care in the future, my friend.
Beware the captains of industry,
For they will rule our world one day,
Ushering in a world of unscrupulous villainy.

The plutocrats are on the move.
Controlling, cajoling, and secretly enrolling.
The super wealthy will soon rule our world,
Dictating, dominating, and all controlling.

Money is the new course of politics.
Governments all will eventually bend the knee.
Democracy will die a slow and painful death;
The signs are there for all to see.

Money is the source of all power.
Money is the new high-powered ideology.
Money motivates and is a powerful weapon;
The super rich are well-armed with technology.

These bloodsuckers have no social responsibilities.
They look on compassion as something strange and funny.
The worship of money is their only philosophy;
In their world the only god is money.

Beware the billionaires of this world,
For they have already inherited the Earth.
Plutocracy, in time, will enslave us all.
They greedily count their billions to see how much they're worth!

They use their power to serve their own purposes.
Increasing poverty and nurturing class conflict,
They will corrupt society with greed and hedonism
While the welfare state lies derelict.

Beware of the future, my friend.
Beware the bloodsucking plutocrats,
For they will rule our world one day
While the poor will live like rats.

Beware the tyranny of wealth.
Beware the tyranny of a plutocracy,
For it plans to rule all our lives
And sound the death knell of democracy.

Inequality is the new watchword of the rich.
The effects on democracy are starting to tell.
The super wealthy are now the ruling class,
And the hapless poor can all go to hell!

The Misery of Slavery

I was like a slave rebelling against his master
when I threw off the chains of slavery.
I no longer wanted to live a life of servitude,
And smoked my last cigarette many years ago.
I admit it wasn't easy,
But I had to sever the chains.
I thought I enjoyed smoking.
I believed it helped to relax me.
I convinced myself it was good for me.
The irony of it …
The drug nicotine ruled my life.
I associated cigarettes with coffee.
I associated coffee with cigarettes.
How could I have a coffee without a cigarette?
How could I have a cigarette without a coffee?
The pleasure I got when I lit one up
And drew the tobacco smoke deep into my lungs:
I was a full-blown addict.
I would have sold my own grandmother for a smoke.
I was pathetic and filled with self-loathing
As my life became a series of small puffs of smoke.
Doing impressions of steam trains.
Blowing smoke rings into the air.
Polluting my lungs and damaging my health.
My breathing was wheezy;
I knew it was slowly killing me …
I then made the decision to quit.
I had quit many times before.
But this time I knew I'd had enough.
Like a slave overthrowing his master
And throwing off the chains of slavery—I quit!
I am as free as a bird.
No more a slave to nicotine!

Memories of India

I wish I could explain why,
But I have an overwhelming desire to return to India,
A mystical and ancient land that lies far to the East,
Where the origins of civilisation marinate in time.
From the Indus Valley to the mighty Ganga River,
It's no wonder India is forever in my memory …
This is my India.
Childhood memories come flooding back;
my love of the sitar and tabla are easily explained.
The smells, scents, and aroma of India are everywhere,
And the hypnotic rhythm of Indian music, which I love.
A hot and humid land with tigers, elephants, and King Cobras,
Brahma bulls, water buffalo, langur monkeys, and pariah dogs.
Ganesh, the elephant-headed Hindu god of beginnings,
The Hindu festival of Dussehra and sacred cows …
This is my India.
A land of aromatic street foods and delicious curries,
Crowds of people buying and selling, hurrying and scurrying.
Trains with barred windows and charwallas furiously selling tea,
along with *punkahwallahs* and *dhobiwallahs*, all etched in my memory.
Clove-scented cigarettes, hibiscus flowers, and garlands of flowers.
Black and yellow taxis stream through the streets of Kolkata.
Monsoon rains fill deep storm drains in seconds.
Turbaned Sikhs, Maharajahs, and the scent of perfumed incense …
This is my India.
Sacred statues covered in garlands of marigolds,
The heady scent of burning incense wafting lazily in the air.
The rhythmic pulse of the tabla, the sweetness of rambutans.
The sacred majesty that is the Himalayas with their soaring heights,
Steep-sided jagged peaks and alpine glaciers of colossal size.
Memories of pony rides and the swirling
mountain mists of Darjeeling …
This is my India, forever in my memory.

The Lifeboat

The ocean appears calm as the lifeboat sets out,
slithering, snakelike, through raging waves.
Sea spray stings reddened eyes as the boat comes about,
And the six men row like galley slaves.

They can see a shimmering light far on the other side.
It beckons them to uncharted shores.
The sea bucks and rolls like an insane roller-coaster ride
As they pull hard on the straining oars.

The sea is churning, and the waves seem to gloat
As the lifeboat is tossed to and fro like a top.
There are six brave men in the flimsy boat,
And each man vows he will never stop.

Their backs are aching, every muscle tight,
As the dark–blue silvery waves divide.
They row with all their strength throughout the night,
With death at their elbows on the deep blue tide.

Exhausted but awake and not fearing the risk,
Each man heaves on his rough-hewn oars.
The boat's forward motion is fast and brisk
As they near those distant shores.

The sea this night wants its revenge
As they try in vain to reach the shore.
The lightning is fierce, and the icy wind howls
As deafening as any hurricane's roar.

The storm's anger suddenly turns to scorn,
And they die at their oars so brave.
And we who survive, we lament and mourn
For those brave men no one could save …

The sea took their lives on that distant shore,
they were lost as the tide slowly turned.
The storm broke and becalmed once more
While dark clouds fled, and the sun returned.

As those who mourn look toward the skies,
Where the morning sun breaks in flames,
Those that knew them lament their demise,
And we who live on will remember their names.

Hidden Valley

Think of a sprawling, hidden valley
Where dwell the screeching devils of old,
Lost souls wandering in the wilderness,
Shrieking their protests against the cold.

God never goes there when the bushfires burn,
But here and there amid smouldering embers,
Gnarled, ancient trees creak nervously,
And the ghost of the past remembers.

At night, the silence is deafening.
Withered gum trees sway in solidarity
With a wisdom of bare-nosed wombats,
Whose muffled grunts are heard with hefty clarity.

Harsh cries echo across a Palaeolithic land,
And a murder of crows caw in happy union
While a troop of wallabies nervously nibble at the grass,
And the river drifts towards its oceanic reunion.

Far above, a wedge-tailed eagle soars motionless,
Eyeing movement at the crest of a precipice
While the yellow wattlebird with its harsh, raucous call
Flits to the nearest tree, joining a nervous exodus.

Hidden where the river lovingly embraces the sea,
The valley hides a magical realm where beauty surrounds.
A lone, craggy mountain watches over the river and valley,
Where life exists forever, and nature abounds.

The Golden Years

When I was young and easy with the world,
I shared stories about youthful antics and happy discoveries.
The green leaves waved gently above my head,
And the green grass swayed beneath my feet.
Were they ever a verdant symphony,
Glistening green, breath of the earth.
Time to savour and time to reflect,
Now, as the golden leaves gently fall
And spiral slowly down to earth.
I look deeply into life's tired eyes
And honour those who didn't make it.
Among the also-ran, I lay,
King of all I could comprehend.
Once, I visualised the trees and leaves
But painted them in black and white.
No bright colours of purple and pink,
No blues or vivid hues, just the dullest grey.
Down the road of life, I struggled
Into the bright lights of summer.
I was young and carefree; I was among friends.
Then came the colours brightly singing as colours do.
Far from home, I was unafraid, I understood.
Colours of bright azure blue, violet, and purple, too.
Magenta, burnt umber, and ultramarine blue,
Cadmium red, yellow, and orange.
Into the sun I ran, joyous and free.
You are young once only,
So, enjoy your life to the full.
But never forget the golden years
Which are far, far closer than you might think.

The Wings of Armageddon

The tempest came like a thief in the night, swirling,
The rain hammering like bullets on the tin roof.
The wind grew in strength, whipping and whirling;
Our humble shelter was anything but bombproof.

Wild and with gusto the storm heaved and crashed,
Sounding like the wings of Armageddon, alas.
Then, a stronger assault, more fierce than the last,
Shook the windows and rattled the glass.

Screaming like some demented Irish banshee,
The wind came renewed, animated, invigorated.
It crashed hard like a rogue wave on rocks,
Angry, tempestuous, and frustrated.

And then, when we'd thought it spent and gone,
It hurled itself anew and attacked once again.
It pounded at the walls and violently shook them
And rattled the rusting tin roof with even-heavier rain.

Howling like the wings of Armageddon,
It ripped off the roof with a single gust
And flung the walls abroad and lifted bricks,
So hateful was its anger, so vile its disgust.

Then, like some soaring raptor, it turned and flew away,
Having finally slated its lust for aggression,
Leaving a trail of destruction in its wake
And howling like the wings of Armageddon.

Rage

Stand fast, stand firm, and never, ever yield,
For you are worth more than you can ever know.
Stand true, stand steady, and never surrender,
For yours is the right to flourish and grow.

Rage at the lack of opportunities.
Rage and never let them forget you.
Rage against any assault on decency,
Even as they tighten the screw.

Take heart, do not despair, and keep up the fight,
For heroes wiser than you and I are here.
Stand fast, stand true, and never yield
As the fight goes on year after oppressive year.

Rage at the corruption of tyrants.
Rage and make sure they hear you.
Rage against any assault on democracy,
Even though your life may be through.

Take strength, stay calm, and fight on, my friend,
For we will win the battle one day.
Trust in honesty, truth, and justice;
For the righteous, there is no other way.

Rage at the curse of inequality.
Rage at the plutocrats of our time.
Rage against the lack of compassion,
Rage at poverty and crime.

Turn, turn towards the light, good people.
Throw off the shackles, break free from your cage.
Evil men will succeed when the good do nothing,
So, you must continue to rage, rage, rage!

Forgotten Dreams

Without warning, I was swallowed by a swirling haze,
Inching ever slowly into the dark and gloomy deep.
My whole body was numb as I moved on in a daze,
Stumbling on fully conscious, yet in a deep sleep.

As my body ascended skyward, I became confused.
I was soaring over mountains tops high and steep.
Buffeting winds left me feeling battered and bruised,
Across haunted valleys, both narrow and deep.

I flew on like an eagle, soaring through the clouds.
Over rivers, lakes, and hillsides lying far beneath,
I flew ever onwards, passing many thunderclouds;
I flew low and passed them underneath.

Around me lay the wrecks of many a forgotten dream,
While deep in my psyche lay a fearful dread
When I heard the sounds of a mournful scream
And thankfully awoke to find I was still in my bed.

Let Me Sing You a Love Song

Let me sing you a song under the apple tree,
The finest song you will have ever heard,
A song about unrequited love and loss,
A song about true love deferred.

Let me sing you a song by the mill pond,
A song to make you think of me,
A song all about a true love,
A song to make your sad heart merry.

Let me sing you a song at the carnival,
A felicitous song to make you dance,
A song to brighten any sad heart,
A song of love's true romance.

Let me sing you a song at daybreak,
A song as bright as the early morning sun,
A song which will make your heart ache,
A song just for you, my precious one.

Let me sing you a song in the garden
Where the deep-red roses grow,
Let me gift you a single red rose,
On my one true love, this I would bestow.

Let me sing you a love song forever
To mend your broken heart.
Let me sing you a sad song of love,
And may we never again be apart.

Growing Old

The term *senior citizens* is such a vacuous phrase:
Respected older citizens? I think not.
Loitering in God's waiting room, put out to grass,
They shuffle towards their fate and slowly rot.

Sons, daughters, fathers, mothers, sisters, brothers:
They have all known life's trials and sweet sorrow.
Each will focus on what they know and understand,
Living for today, knowing there's no tomorrow.

Reminiscing with memories of past loves and lives,
All but forgotten, they suffer in redundant quiet:
Old soldiers, former teachers, husbands, and wives
Existing only and surviving on the blandest diet.

Ask them what it's like to grow old, and they will say:
It is no fun to lose what we used to take for granted.
We've lost the magic twinkle that flickered in the eye
And now live among the dispirited and disenchanted.

We've forgotten what it's like to feel our strength
As each aching limb gets stiffer and stiffer.
The decline is unstoppable, we're going down fast:
Our mental faculties are diminished, and now we're all a dither.

All we can do is mourn the loss of time past,
We are frozen within, occupied by icy winter,
Totally exhausted, and suffering from incontinence:
Our former selves are frozen in the depths of midwinter.

When you are old and grey and life is all but over,
If you're honest and promise to tell the truth:
There are many things you will miss more than ever,
But what you miss more than anything is your youth.

Mannalargenna

His dark eyes are smouldering red,
Yet the fire sticks no longer burn.
Orange ochre once decorated his head
As he mourns a past that can never return.

He lifts his eyes toward the blood-red skies
Where the rising sun breaks aflame.
A deep sadness is reflected in his eyes,
And all but a few have forgotten his name.

When ancient warriors' spears dripped red,
And the dead lay forsaken and quite still,
You'd do well to remember that to survive,
You had to hunt, and you had to kill.

A chieftain proud, a leader of a unique race,
He watched as his people were all but slain.
His fight for freedom was no disgrace;
Across the centuries we still feel his pain.

Distant memories have long since faded,
But his descendants continue to thrive.
Though his memory may now be jaded,
His people have managed to survive.

Brave warrior, it was for them you fought
And struggled and suffered for your pride.
You fought the Black War which only brought
The end to the many of your people who died.

Mannalargenna, you fought a righteous fight
Against immeasurable odds with panache and flare.
You were the wrath, the storm, the light;
You fought a mighty Empire without a prayer.

Mater et Puer

A gentle smile lit up the young face like a beacon;
The look of wonderment shone as brightly as any star,
The gleaming characteristics of birth and death,
Condemned from the very start to an inevitable end.

Intrigued by the light of the sun, eyes look upward.
The pale signature of hope was there from the start,
Kindled in the womb and forged by inherited forces,
The love brimmed over and was accepted by the child.

And so, the bond was forged with blood and pain,
Marinated in lifelong motherly love and devotion.
Burning brightly like the stars of the universe,
Heaven and hell both melded into one small world.

The generous features as starry as the smile
Imprinted forever on the loving face above,
That familiar smile minted fresh as any coin,
The love that forever links the two inseparables.

A life yet to be lived will rise from this strong bond,
Abstracted from the void we struggle to understand.
There is no greater love, no love more intense,
Than the love of a mother for her child

Mother Goodbye

Why are you still with us, Mother?
Why do you linger so long ...
We all think it's time you went,
It's time that you were gone.

Please, don't think we don't love you,
Please, don't think we don't care.
We've waited years to see this through ...
It's time to go, I swear.

Why do you wait so patiently?
What is it you are waiting for ...
It's time to exit peacefully,
It's time to go before.

It's time to leave this mortal shore,
To soar past Jupiter and Mars.
It's time to pass and be no more ...
Returning peacefully to the stars.

Your dementia has grown worse these days,
We don't know why you linger so long.
We all still love you dearly, Mother ...
But we all agree, it's time that you were gone.

A Timeless Love

I spent the night dreaming of crowded bars,
Far away in foreign lands where tourists drink and curse.
We danced together in a galaxy of sparkling stars,
Thrust unannounced on an unsuspecting universe.

I crawled out of the unconsciousness of sleep,
Having dreamt ethereal dreams of timelessness.
I could see you floating in the endless deep;
It was obvious that you were in some distress.

Conventional traditions were smashed and broken;
What was once hell became heaven as we passed.
Between us not a single word was spoken,
Each knew we had found the other at last.

Let me create and forge the stars anew,
Shattering the heavens with a rousing song.
Undeviating and steadfast in my ardent love for you,
Because I know in my heart our love is strong.

Our love will impress both the foolish and the wise,
And our laughter will set the world in flames,
Written in white clouds across the shining skies,
Entwined within a heart, the spectacle of our names.

Till silence roars and charity plunders,
Till fire freezes and ice catches fire,
Till darkness brightens and a whisper thunders,
You—and you alone—will be my heart's desire.

Then—and only then—in the vast empty spaces
Where foolish mortals invent their gods above,
Our mutual love will reflect in both our faces,
Confirming forevermore, our eternal love.

Together forever our hearts serene,
We shall wander amid the stars above.
Hand in hand in our never-ending dream,
Endlessly sharing our timeless love.

82

Worrying about Wombats

Shuffling like a survivor from some horrific disaster,
A bedraggled wombat limps painfully into view.
Piebald and ragged, suffering in silence,
Tragically their numbers are now few.

Wiry coats, threadbare and worn,
Which look pathetic and even strange
As they shuffle around in the morning sun,
Each creature cursed with the dreaded mange.

Their numbers have fallen as many succumb
To the bloodsucking parasite, *Sarcoptes scabiei.*
Known as "scabies" in humans, the original source;
The disease is horrific, and many wombats die.

Think of the suffering these poor creatures must endure,
Whose only crime was to encounter mankind.
For the dreaded mange is the wombat's curse;
No manner of suffering could be more unkind.

Nature looks on unmoved and without care,
Where life and long suffering becomes ever absurder,
And bloodsucking parasites slash fur bare,
With not a flicker of remorse for their bloody murder.

Let's raise awareness of the wombats' plight;
Find a solution, no matter how complex or tough.
Sympathy won't help, no matter how well intentioned.
Worrying about wombats is simply not enough!

Gone Fishing

A salty challenge lies ahead.
Calm waters, ebbing tide: time to fish.
Hook, line, and sinker at the ready,
A big fat fish my only wish.

Muscles strain as the line is cast,
The thread singing as it loosens away.
The ocean gulps as the bait slowly sinks.
How many fish will I catch today?

Time passes slowly as the bright sea glistens,
Salt spray flies, the vengeful tide peaks;
Angry at my attempt to steal the sea's bounties,
a vindictive westerly shrieks.

The translucent waters, now a tangling drift:
Glass like, ever circling in the morning light,
Mangled by the fierce incoming tide,
Circling menacingly and flowing in plain sight.

Where are the bottom feeding fish?
Where the trevally, flounder, flathead, or bream,
where are the cod, whiting, flake, or sole …
It's enough to make you scream!

Gathering Dust

I dwell on moments from the distant past,
Recalling fond memories from yesterday.
Joyous is the memory of you, as you passed
Like a wisp of windblown gossamer at play.

Through hazy memories, I fondly gaze
At shimmering light that tantalizingly dances,
Teasing, touching, treading carefully in a daze
Past distant memories of broken romances.

Free and as delicate as butterflies aflutter,
My thoughts swirl around my empty head,
Dwelling on the words we liked to utter
And the many superficial things we said.

Gone are the memories, forgotten like myself,
Carefully wrapped, packaged, stored away.
Like so many used books gathering dust on the shelf,
To be gently dusted off and opened another day.

Graveyard of the Gods

The gods are all dead now, stiff and cold,
Now that faith, like a bird, has flown.
The gods are as cold as statues made of gold;
Now they all rest in peace in the dead zone.

Forgotten gods, each one once revered,
Now, together in the graveyard of the gods
Once worshipped dutifully and feared,
A very few surviving against the odds.

No more chants, hymns, or sacrifice,
Ancient priests no longer worship in vain.
No more absolution for sin at a price,
Faith in religion is finally on the wane.

This vestige of superstition is fading fast,
But it's not easy to extinguish the fires.
Religion desperately hangs on to the past,
Promising a salvation that no one requires.

It's time we did away with mindless superstition
Brought on by ignorance which we must cut through.
Do not swallow the lie about a bottomless perdition,
But turn to science and what we know is true.

Meanwhile in the Northeast

I'm here sitting on my sofa, quietly reflecting …
A tough battle has just been won
As the struggles of life seek to overcome us.
Ground-floor opulence masked a nervous tension.
Finding somewhere to live became a priority—
Competition between tenants was not for me.
Thankfully, I used my head
And now sit on my sofa, reflecting.
Here I am, walking on the seashore …
Watching the waves gently lapping at the edge.
The sea birds are fishing and dive for their food,
While honking black swans lazily watch on.
Dried seaweed crunches underfoot.
Here and there, a scattering of seashells, mussels, and coral.
While the sea breeze gently blows through my thinning hair,
I'm here, walking along the seashore …
We are all voting in the nation's elections,
Not sure who to vote for.
Trying to do my civic duty in the cold morning fog
As a chill wind blows lazily across the waters,
And the listless waterfowl watch in idle curiosity.
Dutiful citizens shuffle home after casting their votes,
While I sit in silence, remembering the day.
Here I am, mourning the past …
Memories lost forever, unreachable and unattainable,
Frozen in the icy, unrelenting mists of time.
There, but only just out of reach, a fingertip away,
To be unearthed when the time suits, and fondly remembered.
A lifetime of memories for each and every one of us,
Enraging and engulfing our innermost thoughts.
While I sit here, mourning the past …

The end of life, creeping ever closer
As I slowly age from day to day towards life's termination.
The end—the bitter end—draws near
While I sit here, fearing the manner of my inevitable death.

Radiance

Radiant and scorching, the summer sun glowed;
Friends at the beach enjoyed the sun and salty spray.
The grey-green waves lapped as the ocean flowed,
While on sand-encrusted beach towels, we lay.

Swimmers braved the steel-blue rim of the ocean,
Swimming over frightened fish that flashed away.
A lone basking shark swam past with no sign of emotion,
Its cavernous mouth stretched open like some vast antechamber.

We ran headlong into the sea with excited cries,
Leaping gleefully into the sparkling, windswept sea.
Foaming white spray was flung into the azure-blue skies,
Surrounded by the deep-blue ocean eternally.

The calm ocean basked in the afternoon sunshine
As long-nosed fur seals stole nervously ashore.
Clouds fluttered lazily across the rugged coastline
As if they'd often passed this way before.

As the sun sank slowly into the western sea,
Pink clouds danced across the Apple Isle.
The wind was content just to let them be,
While we enjoyed the radiant evening and sat awhile.

We talked and talked as the night crept near,
Stars glittered, and like smiling eyes, were kind.
The radiant moon shone loud and clear;
The hapless sea was now completely blind.

And so, we frolicked beneath the dancing moon,
All night we partied beside the heaving sea.
Alas, the night was over and all too soon,
For we were young back then, and we were free.

Mumirimina People

The Mumirimina people from Tasmania
Once travelled these ancient trade routes.
The Kutalayna River flowed between the Big River
And the Oyster Bay Aboriginal tribal groups.

Collecting ochre and making stone tools,
Keeping alive their customs and hopes,
Feasting on shellfish or birds and their eggs,
Seeking reeds to make baskets and ropes.

Life was simple for the Mumirimina people.
Nature provided much in numerous ways.
They hunted kangaroo, wallaby, or possum,
On their lands where sheep now graze.

The Jordan Valley was a favourite hunting ground
Where the Oyster Bay people gathered food
With their close allies, the Big River tribe;
Their close collaboration was strong and good.

Then came the white men from afar,
And the first of many massacres took place.
Many died or were driven from their homes;
Some disappeared without trace.

The settlers clashed with the Aborigines,
Many innocents were killed on both sides.
A tragic clash of cultures or genocide?
It spelled the end for many ancient tribes.

Without You

Without you, I am nothing.
You are the love of my life,
My very soul, my happiness,
My sweetheart, best friend, and wife.

Without you, I am in darkness.
You are my shining light.
You are the stars in my sky,
You are my day and my night.

Without you, I am lost.
It was love from the start.
You are my joy; you are my treasure,
The very beat of my heart.

Without you, I am dead.
I'm grateful for the love you bring.
You are my world, my universe;
You are my everything.

The Middle Kingdom Maze

Looking back, it all seems like a distant dream
When my thoughts go back to my China days.
Happy days and days when I could scream,
Living in the Middle Kingdom maze.

Contrasting customs, language impotence,
Smiling faces, inscrutable ways.
No point sitting on the fence,
It was time to explore, time to appraise.

Cities unfurl in an endless sprawl,
Soaring tower blocks defying gravity.
Stories of dynastic rise and fall,
A history of invention and depravity.

Rivers carve their presence across the land,
Past ancient temples and burning incense,
Bonsai trees skilfully grown by hand,
Temple monks studying the art of self defence.

An ancient thread of journeys, along a silken road
Where the Great Wall trails like a dragon's spine.
Where demons dance at a cultural crossroad,
An elaborate maze woven with the threads of time.

China is now just a fading memory.
Happy memories to last me all my days,
Filled with riches like an Emperor's treasury.
How I miss my time in the Middle Kingdom maze!

The Power of Trees

From the frozen north to tropical rain forests,
Trees are captivating and vibrantly alive.
The world's trees should never be taken for granted—
We need them to prosper, and ultimately, thrive.

Sitting on a grassy hill under the shade of large trees,
I reflect on how trees are sanctuaries for wildlife.
The background of many a happy memory,
Trees have been with me my entire life.

Trees hold tremendous powers and ask very little.
They are silent and watchful, like dutiful sentinels,
A welcome patch of green our eyes often seek out—
The thought of a world without trees is untenable.

Trees make all our lives better and healthier.
If a tree has power, a forest has even more.
Some trees are up to four thousand years old.
To beat greenhouse gases, we need trees galore.

Climate change will eventually kill us all,
Unless we use trees to store carbon dioxide.
The atmosphere has been warming our planet—
Without trees, our planet will soon die.

We need smarter management of trees.
Trees look out for us, so we must look out for trees.
By planting new trees, we will conserve and protect.
We must save our trees; do help us, please!

Murderous Attack

A hoarse, authoritative voice yelled out a command: "For-ward!"
Slowly at first, we advanced.
Onward toward our foe, eager to kill.
A machine gun barked.
The bullets spat out.

The machine gunner grabbed another clip;
He quickly reloaded and fired again.
Bullets sped, hissing, into the grey-clad forms that loomed ahead,
Mowing them down.
They tried to surrender, but death harvested them.
We went at them with bayonets and trenching spades.
We trampled bloodied bodies.
We slipped in spilled intestines.
We butchered our fellow humans with our bare hands.
Kill, soldier, kill for your country and freedom!
But we will never be free.
We live with the memories still,
Forever haunted by the dreadful scenes of our murderous attack.

Listening to Pine Trees

You are surrounded by green trees;
They teeter in the wind as if ready to topple.
You stand in their midst in wonderment,
Like a king looking at his gold.
Underfoot lie the pine needles of yesteryear.

Long dead, they rustle when you walk on them
;
They smell of the forest and nature
As you tiptoe respectfully by.
The swaying pine trees make little noise,
But if you lift your head, you can hear them talk.
They whisper as they whip the air

In a futile effort to make you understand.
But you do not listen to the pine trees,
And their message goes unheeded
While you stand, ignorant, in their midst
Like a fool looking at his navel.
Life is Short

We live our short lives on the other side of the veil,
Wondering endlessly at the mysteries of time
Which passes quickly as we grow old and frail,
Only to become sacrificial lambs on some blood-soaked shrine.

For we were once young, so many years ago …
It is said that with age comes wisdom.
The absolute truth is we will never really know,
If we never think to question the omnipresent system.

We are dead a long time, dead for an eternity,
And nothing will be known of us, not even our name.
Our lives forgotten like some badly whistled song,
And extinguished like a flickering flame.

We all will die before our song takes flight …
Never more to live our lives for living's sake.
We live in hope and die in fear at night;
Life is short and then we die, never again to wake.

As we pass, a silent sigh gently stirs,
And we slide forever into the gloom.
Death comes swiftly with its promise of rest,
And there comes a deathly silence in the room.

Mourn me not, for I have answered the call …
The silence of eternity is now all mine.
To rest in peace should time ever fall,
and vanish quickly like the passing of time.

The Business of Wombats

What a wonderfully weird creature is the wombat!
Short-legged and stocky but by no means fat,
With a stubby little tail and a very cute gait,
I may see a wombat, if I lie patiently in wait.

I'm watching near a burrow and here I quietly lie,
And if I'm very lucky, a wombat may pass by.
They are not often seen as they are painfully shy,
I so much want to see a wombat saunter by!

They have rat-like front teeth and powerful claws,
And wombats are protected under each state's laws.
I love to observe them and adore their strange ways
As they venture out to feed on cool or overcast days.

Like many other marsupials, wombats have pouches;
They're mostly friendly but can occasionally be grouches.
Wombats are special, and to me, they're really cool dudes.
Can you name another animal that does its business in cubes?

I Am Lost

My pig brain doubles as a mentor
As the sea sucks the land.
I live in a hollow hulk,
Swallowed whole by the establishment.
I still hear my father's voice
As he believes the improbable.
Mum put up with it all
As she played bingo on the weekends,
Tomorrow's driver in her brand-new car,
Bisected shadows in the stairwell,
Convinced that the unborn had the right to life.
Corrosive milk sprouted from her teats
While the baby bled and babbled,
For love was lost from the beginning,
And the unplanned ghosts lay smashed in the gutter
While the cripple clutched his crutch,
Limping under the gas lamps
Among the rubble of an air-raid.
At stake were the sleepers in their savage graves,
Unmourned and unmissed;
Even the clergy laughed.
The infected calves were slaughtered as they suckled
While the pigs looked on from the trees,
Sucking in the dark, kissing the feet of the unwashed.
What colour is death?
All at once, there's sanity,
Piercing point of putrefaction
Pricking the consciences of the clergy
As they line up, heaven bound,
While the dumb queue up to believe their crap.
The birds have all flown away
While the bandaged mummy weeps for the past.
The desert has wilted, and shade is at a premium.

Egypt is now on the bucket list;
I still hope to go there one day.
My world was once in an English valley;
Now, I hear through dead men's voices,
Tricked into opening my bowels daily.
My grave is close at hand,
Near the dead house on the plain.
The markings on my skin reveal my inner thoughts.
I turn and see them as they swivel,
Worshipping the orange devil,
Cursed and bleeding from his ears.
Am I alone?
Who knows the bitter taste of death?
What colour is glory?

I am lost.
To My Grandson, Finn

In the early days, when you first drew breath and cried,
Proudly, I watched you grow up from afar.
I felt so grateful and had an expectant sense of pride.
To those of us who loved you, you were a star.

From the moment you were born, I loved you.
In truth, as soon as I knew you were expected,
I knew you were blessed with a loving family,
Who would love you and keep you protected.

There are no words to express how much you mean to me.
Your birth has given me a whole new sense of joy,
Because, until you were born, I always thought it would be
That I'd never know a grandson: a special, precious boy.

Remember with respect those that brought you here.
Your ancestors who laboured with ardent diligence,
Their sacrifices made you who and what you are, my dear.
I know they would love you in all your perfect innocence.

Tightly grasp the baton as into the future you stride.
Generations past walk with you, still dreaming.
Always remember, Finn, that you are watched with pride.
Grow strong and prosper and show us all that life has meaning.

About the Author

Photo by Marianne Hender.

Leslie Hender is a published author and is best described as cosmopolitan. Born in Hong Kong, his father was an engineer, which meant the family was fortunate enough to live in such faraway places as Malaysia, India, Nepal, Germany, and Belgium.

Because of his upbringing, he acquired a lasting interest in different cultures, culminating in an extended trip to China, where he taught English for thirteen years and met his current wife, June. Leslie has a unique sense of humour, which is reflected in some of his poems. He is also passionate about the importance of justice and equity, which can also be found in his poetry.

Leslie comes from a creative background, having worked as a creative copywriter for many years. After he retired, he and his wife, June, made the decision to settle in Tasmania, where they could enjoy the peace and tranquility, as well as the uniqueness of this very special island.